Space

Nick Hunter

www.raintreepublishers.co.uk
Visit our website to find out more information about Raintree books.

To order:
☎ Phone 0845 6044371
🖹 Fax +44 (0) 1865 312263
🖳 Email myorders@raintreepublishers.co.uk

Customers from outside the UK please telephone +44 1865 312262

Raintree is an imprint of Capstone Global Library Limited, a company incorporated in England and Wales having its registered office at 7 Pilgrim Street, London, EC4V 6LB – Registered company number: 6695582

Text © Capstone Global Library Limited 2013

First published in hardback in 2013
The moral rights of the proprietor have been asserted.

Edited by Rebecca Rissman, Dan Nunn, and Catherine Veitch
Designed by Cynthia Della-Rovere
Levelling by Jeanne Clidas
Picture research by Elizabeth Alexander
Production by Victoria Fitzgerald
Originated by Capstone Global Library
Printed and bound in China by CTPS

ISBN 978 1 406 24190 7
16 15 14 13 12
10 9 8 7 6 5 4 3 2 1

British Library Cataloguing in Publication Data
Hunter, Nick
Space. -- (Explorer tales)
919.9'04-dc22
A full catalogue record for this book is available from the British Library.

Acknowledgements
We would like to thank the following for permission to reproduce photographs: Alamy pp. 9 (© Peter Horree), 11 (© RIA Novosti), 13 (© ITAR-TASS Photo Agency), 17 (© AF archive), 27 (© Pictorial Press Ltd); Corbis p. 24 (© Stocktrek Images); Getty Images pp. 8 (NASA), 10 (Keystone/Hulton Archive), 12 (Bates Littlehales/National Geographic), 14 (SSPL), 15 (Time Life Pictures/NASA); NASA pp. 7, 16, 19 (Sandra Joseph and Kevin O'Connell), 18, 20, 21, 22 (JPL-Caltech), 23 (JPL-Caltech), 25; Science Photo Library p. 26 (Steve Gschmeissner); Shutterstock pp. 4 (© Nikm), 5 (© Sebastian Kaulitzki), 6 (© Anteromite).

Cover photographs of an astronaut reproduced with permission of Shutterstock (© eddtoro); Northern and Southern Celestial hemisphere, 1880, reproduced with permission of Sanders of Oxford, rare prints & maps (www.sandersofoxford.com); Saturn reproduced with permission of NASA (JPL). Background design features of the solar system reproduced with permission of Shutterstock (© Anteromite).

Every effort has been made to contact copyright holders of material reproduced in this book. Any omissions will be rectified in subsequent printings if notice is given to the publisher.

Disclaimer
All the internet addresses (URLs) given in this book were valid at the time of going to press. However, due to the dynamic nature of the internet, some addresses may have changed, or sites may have changed or ceased to exist since publication. While the author and publisher regret any inconvenience this may cause readers, no responsibility for any such changes can be accepted by either the author or the publisher.

Contents

Journey to the stars 4
What is space? 6
Into space 8
First person in space 10
How do you land a rocket? 12
Man on the Moon 14
"The Eagle has landed" 16
The Space Shuttle 18
Living in space 20
Exploring the Solar System 22
Mission to Mars 24
Life on other planets? 26
Timeline 28
Becoming an astronaut 29
Glossary 30
Find out more 31
Index 32

Some words are shown in bold, **like this**. You can find out what they mean by looking in the glossary.

Journey to the stars

For thousands of years, people looked at the night sky and told stories about the **stars**. Since 1961, space explorers, or astronauts, have risked their lives to discover what lies beyond Earth.

The **ancient** Greeks arranged the stars into groups that looked like characters from stories. This is Orion the Hunter.

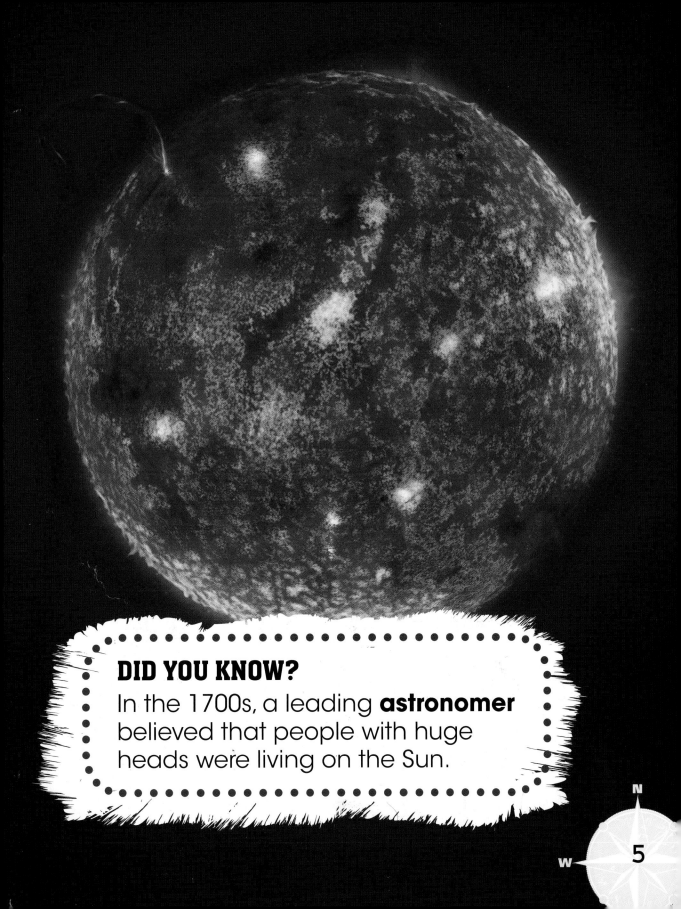

DID YOU KNOW?

In the 1700s, a leading **astronomer** believed that people with huge heads were living on the Sun.

What is space?

Space is closer than you think. Earth is surrounded by a layer of **gases**. Beyond this layer is space. In space we can see the Moon, the **planets** of our **solar system**, and some of the billions of **stars**.

Earth

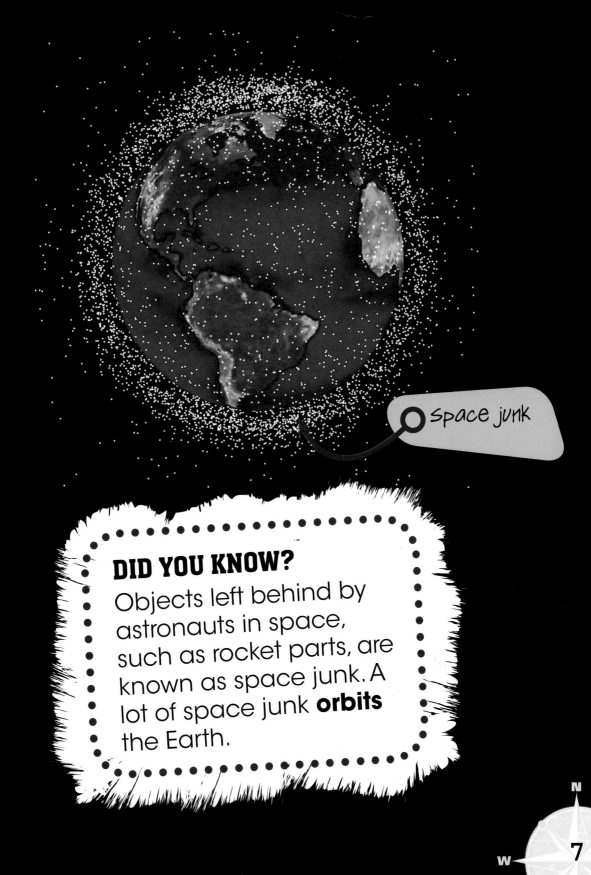

space junk

DID YOU KNOW?
Objects left behind by astronauts in space, such as rocket parts, are known as space junk. A lot of space junk **orbits** the Earth.

Into space

After take-off, spacecraft travel around nine times faster than a speeding bullet. Astronauts wear special suits to protect them in space. If you left a spacecraft without wearing a spacesuit, you would not survive for long.

First person in space

On 12 April 1961, Russian astronaut Yuri Gagarin blasted into space. Gagarin was the first human space explorer. His spaceflight lasted only 108 minutes. It nearly ended in disaster when two sections of Gagarin's spacecraft failed to separate correctly.

Laika was the first dog sent into space.

DID YOU KNOW?

Several animals were sent into space before Gagarin, including a dog and two monkeys.

How do you land a rocket?

Spacecraft are travelling at thousands of kilometres per hour when they re-enter Earth's **atmosphere**. The first US spacecrafts used **parachutes** to slow down before landing in the sea.

parachute

In 1963, Valentina Tereshkova was the first woman in space. Before becoming an astronaut, her hobby was parachuting.

Man on the Moon

On 16 July 1969, the *Apollo 11* spacecraft lifted off on its way to the Moon. The astronauts travelled nearly 386,242 kilometres to reach the Moon.

Michael Collins trains for his flight on *Apollo 11*.

DID YOU KNOW?

A modern mobile phone has a more powerful computer than the spacecraft that took astronauts to the Moon.

Apollo 11

"The Eagle has landed"

Those were Neil Armstrong's words as *Apollo 11* landed on the Moon. Armstrong and "Buzz" Aldrin became the first humans to step foot on another world. Michael Collins remained on *Apollo 11* as it **orbited** the Moon.

Buzz Aldrin

A film starring Tom Hanks was made about the *Apollo 13* mission.

DID YOU KNOW?

Only 12 astronauts have ever set foot on the Moon. *Apollo 13* failed to get there after an explosion.

The Space Shuttle

The space shuttle was launched in 1981. Blasting off while attached to the shuttle's fuel tanks was like being attached to a huge bomb. The rocket boosters could not be stopped until the fuel ran out.

drag chute

fuel tank

rocket booster

DID YOU KNOW?
The space shuttle was the first spacecraft that could be used more than once.

Living in space

Space shuttle missions carried parts to build an International Space Station. Astronauts on the space station are doing experiments to help future space explorers.

The International Space Station is around the size of a football pitch.

jet pack

DID YOU KNOW?
Astronauts use jet packs to move around on a spacewalk.

Exploring the Solar System

Humans have only explored the parts of space closest to Earth. The *Voyager* spacecraft have travelled to the end of our **solar system**, but not with astronauts on board.

Unmanned space rovers have explored the surface of the **planet** Mars.

DID YOU KNOW?

Mars is home to the biggest volcano in the solar system.

Mission to Mars

The **planet** Mars is the next target for space explorers. It would take at least a year to travel to Mars and back.

Long periods of **weightlessness** in space can damage the human body's bones and muscles. Exercising in space is important to help stop the damage.

Life on other planets?

Space explorers have not found life anywhere else in space. If there is life in our **solar system**, it is likely to be simple life like **bacteria**.

bacteria

There are billions of **planets** in space. Do you think one of them could be home to alien beings like the ones we see in films and on TV?

Timeline

1957   4 October: *Sputnik 1* is the first craft in space.

3 November: Laika the dog is the first living passenger on a spacecraft.

1961   12 April: Yuri Gagarin becomes the world's first astronaut.

1963   16 June: Valentina Tereshkova becomes the first woman in space.

1969   20 July: Neil Armstrong is the first person to walk on the Moon.

17 April: *Apollo 13* mission returns safely to Earth after an explosion during its mission to the Moon.

1981   12 April: Launch of the first space shuttle mission from the Kennedy Space Center in Florida, USA.

Becoming an astronaut

Thousands of people apply every year to become astronauts. Only a lucky few are selected.
To become an astronaut you need to:

- study hard in maths or science
- be physically fit
- be an experienced military pilot
- be brave enough to journey into the unknown.

Have you got what it takes?

Glossary

ancient lived or existed a long time ago

astronomer someone who studies space

atmosphere layer of gases that surrounds Earth

bacteria tiny living things that can only be seen with a microscope

gas substance, such as air, that has no fixed shape

orbit path along which something moves around a planet or other body in space

parachute large piece of fabric that slows someone down when falling from an aircraft

planet large ball of rock or gas that orbits a star, the way our planet Earth goes around the Sun

solar system collection of planets and other bodies that go around the Sun

star huge ball of burning gas that produces massive amounts of heat and light

weightlessness when someone floats in the air, as astronauts do in space

Find out more

Books

Astronaut (321 Go!), Steve Rickard (Ransom, 2010)

Spacecraft (Machines Close-Up), Daniel Gilpin (Wayland, 2010)

Who Walks in Space?: Working in Space (Wild Work), Linda Tagliaferro (Raintree, 2011)

Websites

school.discoveryeducation.com/ schooladventures/spacestation/
Find out more about the amazing International Space Station.

www.kidsastronomy.com/index.htm
Learn lots of facts about the Solar System on this website.

www.nasa.gov/audience/forkids/kidsclub/ flash/index.html
Games, videos, and lots of information from NASA, the organization in charge of US space exploration.

Index

alien life 26, 27
animals in space 11
Apollo spacecraft
  14–17
Armstrong, Neil 16
astronauts 4, 7, 8–10,
  13, 14, 16–17, 20,
  21, 29
astronomers 5
atmosphere 12

bacteria 26

Gagarin, Yuri 10
gases 6
Greeks, ancient 4

International Space
  Station 20

jet packs 21

Mars 23, 24
Moon 6, 14, 16, 17

parachutes 12
planets 6, 23, 24, 27

rocket boosters 18,
  19

solar system 6, 22,
  23, 26
space junk 7
space rovers 23
space shuttle
  18–19, 20
spacesuits 8, 9
spacewalks 21
stars 4, 6
Sun 5

Tereshkova,
  Valentina 13

Voyager 22

weightlessness 25